Retired Women—
Laughing at Gravity

Sheila Lopez

iUniverse, Inc.
Bloomington

Retired Women—Laughing at Gravity

iUniverse books may be ordered through booksellers or by contacting:

iUniverse
1663 Liberty Drive
Bloomington, IN 47403
www.iuniverse.com
1-800-Authors (1-800-288-4677)

Because of the dynamic nature of the Internet, any web addresses or links contained in this book may have changed since publication and may no longer be valid.
Any people depicted in stock imagery provided by Thinkstock are models, and such images are being used for illustrative purposes only.

Certain stock imagery © Thinkstock.

ISBN: 978-1-4620-0736-3 (sc)
ISBN: 978-1-4620-0737-0 (ebk)

Printed in the United States of America

iUniverse rev. date: 4/6/2011

For Laughing Sue.

And in the sweetness of friendship,
let there be laughter and sharing of pleasure.
—Aristotle

Contents

Acknowledgments

Many thanks to "My Girlfriends' Garden" women's support group in Auburn, California, for encouraging us all to follow our passions—just for the fun of it!

Thank God for girlfriends.

Introduction

Dear Retired Women Everywhere,

As a psychotherapist for thirty years, I spent at least thirty thousand hours with clients, talking about the meaning of life. People often heard laughter emanating from the therapy room and said, "They're having too much fun in there!"

How could the heartache and confusion that prompted people to seek professional help possibly be funny? Such is the wonder of the human spirit! For thirty years I learned, along with my clients, the secret of good mental health in any chapter of life: *It's all in how you look at it.*

Now I am in the retirement chapter of life. Unlike previous chapters in my personal story, this one can be read while lying out in the sun—what difference will it make to my skin now?

The characters in the retirement chapter of my life may have lost skin elasticity, a bit of height, and the willingness to look into a magnifying mirror, but they have gained the freedom to watch a movie at lunchtime, write their memoirs, and laugh at the strangest things.

I have no need for cosmetic surgery when I look into the seasoned faces of the girls over fifty who fill my retired days with intrigue and fun. Watching them, I can see that the secrets to beauty in this chapter of life are simple: we must use our laugh lines by laughing, brighten our eyes with love and respect for others, and stand as straight and tall as possible while walking into our future with joy and gratitude.

So come along, join hands, and let's laugh at gravity!

Chapter 1

FASHION TRADE SECRETS

Trading fashion secrets with our peers began early. Remember high school when we rolled our bobby socks down to our ankles? For a while our dads' white dress shirts hung to the knees of our rolled-up jeans. We powdered our white buck shoes. We experimented with blue eye shadow and hid our pierced ears from our parents. We plucked each other's eyebrows to a frightening degree. Dyed-to-match sweaters and straight wool skirts were at the top of our Christmas wish lists.

Together, we starched layers of stiff slips to wear under our poodle skirts. We became skilled with bobby pins and slept on nests of pin curls.

As the years passed, we went to tie-dye parties and impersonated hippies by wearing earth mother skirts and blouses.

Later, we slept with our heads balancing on huge rollers and teased our hair into massive, bouffant hairstyles. We learned to use electric curling irons. We gave up perms and went back to them again. We discussed the pros and cons of bright red lipstick versus subtle gloss. We read magazines full of secrets about how to accentuate our best features. We studied mannequins for ideas on how to mix and match our apparel. We spent hours together in front of our bathroom mirrors, preparing our faces for the maddening light-show of the disco.

Through all these growing-up years, nothing was more fun than being girls: banding together in laughing groups to seek beauty and style, so someday we could live the dream of being sophisticated and fashionable wives, mothers, and career women.

Then, something went wrong.

Our "Reality Show"

As young adult women, instead of spending glamorous mornings primping, we found ourselves sponging our kids' oatmeal off the lapels of our pantsuits, shoving earrings into our earlobes while looking for lost homework, and pulling on tall boots to hide our unshaven legs.

Although we dressed as quickly as firefighters each workday, we still had to pay attention to the impressions we made. Think about it: in our working days every garment and accessory was held up to the light of what was "appropriate." There were few things worse for a career than dressing like a teenager; a nun; a drill-sergeant; or, heaven forbid, a hooker!

Accessories that jingled, jangled, or clanked could upset the natural balance of office protocol. We couldn't afford to have our styles judged as seductive, eccentric, vain, ridiculous, over-the-top, or simply, "in denial."

Alas, the age of experimenting with new "looks" was over. We had to fit in, tone down, grow up, blend, and neutralize.

Adulthood ended our fashion freedom.

Sizzle!

This is why I was so excited the first time I shopped with my new, retired girlfriends.

On our first shopping excursion I wore my office attire: slacks with crisp creases, a bright silk blouse, a dependable blazer, and dressy leather boots with sensible heels.

These gals are a few years my senior and are, therefore, more experienced at being retired than I am. Comparing my fashion freedom with theirs, I felt like the matron at a women's prison.

I followed them around the jewelry counter as they gathered long sparkling necklaces and noisy bracelets. I watched them try on jeans with rhinestones on the rear pockets and waistbands hugging their hips.

While I looked for a white blouse with a collar to wear to a retirement luncheon, they chose tight-fitting knit shirts with sequins and lace.

My glamorous role models grabbed up gauzy skirts of many layers. They slipped their bare pedicures into strappy little sandals. They tilted hats with huge flowers and saucy brims on their tinted hair. They adorned their shoulders with sparkling scarves. Names of famous designers tripped off their tongues as easily as names of previous husbands.

May I Introduce ...

These retired women are special; aging has only enhanced their beauty.

One member of our troupe is a retired high-fashion model in her seventies. When we pick her up for an outing, she glides rather than walks out of her mobile home. Head held high, she presents herself like someone on her way to a photo op. Where does she find those long, simple skirts? How does she match the unexpected shades of her flimsy blouses and velvet shawls?

And the jewelry! Her stunning necklaces hypnotize those of us wearing simple lockets and beads. Even her dialogue is high-toned as she dramatically quotes lines from the theatre or simply bestows her own sentiment of the day:

"We are the perfect age for where we are in life!" she says, with a flourish. We who live in a dowdier world can only answer with something profound from the daily horoscope.

A second diva in our group is an eighty-something ex-chorus girl. She kicks up her heels with furs and diamonds bestowed by a loving gentleman friend. Not that she does the can-can for fun these days. This beauty is a portrait of sizzling composure. Her wardrobe is all vanilla and strawberries, if you know what I mean. Her translucent complexion, which by her admission is a product of modern technology, is peaches and cream. She can be described only as "delicious."

The baby of our retired clique is our beautiful German gourmet, in her late fifties. A world traveler, she introduced us to artisan bread with butter and pesto. Her fashion sense revolves around large pieces of stunning family-heirloom jewelry, picked up at flea markets for a song.

Then we have our beautiful, eighty-something belly dancer. A retired legal secretary, she was a plain Jane, she says, until she started dancing. That was around the age of sixty. Beginning with Delilah on videotape, she realized she was physically strong and could move to the music like a cobra. A couple of classes later, she began performing at parties. Eventually, her belly dancer persona evolved into a new, everyday style. Now she even gives lessons.

Inspired, I dance with her around and around in the space between her sofa and her huge television. Together, we march into shops specializing in belly-dancing apparel. With the confidence of desert divas, we pick up sparkling skirts with slits up one side and down the other; halter tops with bells celebrating every shimmying curve; strands of tiny, noisy cymbals to drape around our undulating hips; and noisy bracelets with seductive charms, not only for our wrists but also for our ankles and even our toes!

Dressing in costume for belly dancing fun gives me a different persona too. I realize I like myself as "Sheena."

If Not Now, When?

Guess what? Now that we're retired, how we dress is up for grabs again! Our kids aren't going to hide their heads if we don't dress like the rest of the moms. Our bosses aren't going to write notes about our apparel in our job evaluations. We are free!

But we're a bit out of practice when it comes to dressing for fun instead of function. Changing one's style of dress after decades of oppression is a bit like breaking out of a boring conversation: sometimes the only thing to do is just walk away.

Can we really stack our polyester pantsuits, our good wool skirts, and our corduroy blazers in boxes and haul them off to the donation center? Can we learn to ignore sideways glances from more sedate ladies in our age brackets as we wear glitter and bling? Can we sparkle rather than blend? Can we step out of our comfort zones into choruses of "oohs" and "ahs"?

All this we must ask ourselves, entering our closets as retired women.

Yes, We Can!

Retired women! We must forget our grandmothers' fashion fears. Instead, we must band together as we did in our bobby-socks days and liberate the closets of an entire generation of grandmothers! Together we must adorn, decorate, and celebrate ourselves with fashion!

We must rediscover fashion freedom and spread the word to retired women everywhere: there are new rules for senior grooming:

- Never dress your age.

- Free your hair to grow after fifty.

- Stand out in a crowd.

- Wear your granddaughters' jeans.

- Follow color at sale racks.

- See your own beauty at last!

As I reach across the department store counter and hold a pair of bright, dangling earrings up to my ears, my make-over-artist friends watch in a circle and applaud.

"Can I really wear these in public?" I ask my reflection in the mirror.

"Yes, you can!" they say in a chorus.

And that is the new beginning!

*Our eighty-something belly dancer realized she
could move to the music like a cobra.*

Chapter 2

Hunt and Gather

Retirement is the best time of life to go shopping. As we lock the car and march across the parking lot to the mall, we share the thrill of the hunt. We are young and wild again and on the prowl for a bargain.

"Here we come," our excited chatter announces to hopeful store owners. "We are the seasoned spenders, the clever consumers, the debit card divas!"

Heavy doors open automatically in glad welcome. Strains of hypnotic music serenade our joyful entry. Thousand of bright watts spotlight us. Others may call our love of shopping "materialism," but we know better. Shopping gives us what money can't buy. How do we love it? Let me count the ways:

Merchandise Us

No doubt, the lure of the mall is contrived by psychologists who think they know us better than we know ourselves. The festive music is designed to make us feel young and wealthy. The bright lights blind us to the fact that we don't really need what we're buying. The darling outfit in the window draws us into the store like a magnet, where we discover the anorexic mannequin wears the only size available. What do we care? They never promised us liposuction!

Call us brainwashed, but the smells of chocolate chip cookies baking, coffee drinks steaming, and toasty pretzels floating in midair ease our bouts of fibromyalgia and instantly cure our fatigue syndromes.

Let the clever young market-manipulators work on our psyches. At this time of life we have no fear of mind-bending; our minds are as flexible as our underarms.

Giving up shopping because the thrill is the result of ploys would be like giving up earrings just because our earlobes have stretched an inch or two. Never happen!

Psychotherapy For Free

Group shopping in retirement has tremendous mental health benefits. For example, if a friend repeatedly refuses invitations to shop, the group knows there is something seriously wrong. She may be angry or even depressed; or perhaps she has forgotten who you are. Whatever the case, you must act right away!

If she is angry, it is crucial to get to the bottom of it immediately. Tell her she is loved and that if she's not happy, nobody's happy! Then remind her: senior discount day doesn't last forever.

If she still refuses to shop and her sad demeanor implies she has lost interest in normal pleasurable activities, she may be having a bout of clinical depression. Depression has been shown to actually block the natural, healthy flow of the shopping impulse! Forget therapists and pills, and get the latest sale ads. Two of anything for the price of one is a natural, foolproof antidepressant.

Finally, if it is apparent your friend has forgotten who you are, reintroduce yourselves and get her into a store as soon as possible. Certain mental ailments of older age have been miraculously forestalled by the purchase of a fine set of bath towels!

Female Bonding

The day we retire, we begin calling our women friends "honey," "dear," and "sweetie." When we were young such endearments sounded just plain ridiculous. Now they seem the only way to truly express the depth of our love for the beauty and grace that is a woman friend.

When we're in this mood, every shopping spree is a complicated celebration, full of challenges, because at our ages we are determined not to just "go along" with any activity that makes us wish we were home sweeping the deck.

To pull off a shopping spree in which everyone remains "dear" to everyone else, certain variables must be carefully handled.

When Do We Eat?

We retired women have histories of hungry hearts, hiding behind our weight, using food to blunt our feelings, and so on. It's no wonder that arranging a harmonious lunch hour requires great compromise:

"If no one minds, I'd really like to eat early, before my blood sugar strikes me dumb."

"That's fine, dear, but I do have to consider my milkshake-diet schedule. I pay beaucoup bucks for this program."

"Anytime we eat is okay with me. I'm in a colon cleanse right now, so I'll only be drinking water."

"I have a coupon for 10 percent off. Can we eat before it expires at eleven?"

"I never eat breakfast, but don't worry about me; I'm used to being the skinniest one here."

"Table for five?"

When the handsome young host shows us to a table, he has no idea what an accomplishment it is for us to say, "Yes, thank you."

The Designated Driver

Once the lunchtime is established, the designated driver is chosen. This honor goes to the driver everyone (secretly) feels safest with.

It's not that we fear the driving ability of the friend whose front tires recently landed over a parking curb. We all agree (while taking sideways glances at each other) that the curb was never there before. Besides, she's quite right when she says if they made car tires with a little more bounce, the car could come right back over again without even calling the tow service.

And anyone could get her shoe caught between the gas and brake pedals at a stoplight, making the car ram the back of the car in front. It's absolutely true: they should recall defective shoes like that!

Then there's the issue of the potential driver who is willing to forgo wine with lunch. While it is not nearly as satisfying to toast each other with a cup of tea, someone must be willing to demonstrate our loyalty to Mothers Against Drunk Driving.

Therefore, it is the sober friend who has not lately jumped a curb or rammed a car from behind who is our first choice as designated driver.

The Invitation List

To really work, a shopping spree can include a maximum of five ladies. Five is the number that can fit into the designated driver's car with everyone having a seat belt. Five is the ideal number for warranting a large table at lunch. Five can be broken up into two pairs plus the inevitable loner for dispersing throughout a store before we meet again in thirty minutes.

The trouble comes when two best friends each meets a new best friend she wants to include. This necessitates a doubling of all the equations and may render the shopping spree hopeless.

Getting Along

As we shop with friends, we must keep in mind what years of shopping on the buddy system have taught us:

- When asked if the too-tight pants your friend is trying on make her look you-know-what, simply bring her a chair and suggest she try sitting in them to "make sure they're the right cut."

- When shopping with the "hiker," wear your tennies. She's the one who insists on shopping in stores miles apart and then ends the day with one last trip back to the store you started from.

- Don't leave your car motor running, even if all you intend to do is dash into the store for a refund. Some of the most wonderful shopping sprees are the result of the simple need to return a previously purchased item.

- Ask for separate checks at lunch. Friendships can be seriously strained by the passion of figuring the proper tip.

The Hazards of Hoarding

Of course, with all the shopping trips behind us by the time we retire, it's imperative that we consider the hazards of hoarding.

Let's face it, we must schedule regular trips to the donation center. When we want to cling to that orange tissue dispenser, we must imagine how thrilled the younger woman who buys it will be. Likewise, we are doing a good deed when we allow our vases, picture frames, water glasses, and our perfectly good patent leather pumps to inspire delight in brand-new owners.

We simply *must* let go. We have let go of our sleeveless blouses, our 2.25 reading glasses, and our plastic hair bows. We have even let go, to a great extent, of our adult children. Surely we can let go of our past shopping treasures to make room for the new.

Shop On

Whatever we do, we must not stop shopping:

- Shopping is the "hunting and gathering" of modern womanhood.

- It's the medium with which we hold lifesaving women's support groups.

- Shopping with the girls spares our men hours of bravely staring into space while sitting in a lacy chair near the fitting room.

- Shopping allows us to give each other much-needed makeovers.

- It prevents us from getting into the habit of going everywhere dressed like we are going out to feed the chickens.

- Shopping is fun.

- It is necessary.

- Shopping is the superglue of female relationships!

*When we're in this mood, every shopping
spree is a complicated celebration.*

Chapter 3

Fulfill a Childish Dream

I no longer fear making a fool of myself. After all, one can only be labeled "foolish" by people who are paying attention. At my rapidly advancing age, I finally realize most people are far more interested in discussing the choices at the family-buffet restaurant than they are in discussing me. This awareness gives me a sensation of freedom and lightness similar to the mesmerizing calm of a soak in the hot tub—before the grandkids and dog jump in.

Therefore, I decided to face up to my clinical case of Hostess-Posttraumatic Stress Disorder and throw an unforgettable Christmas tea party for my girlfriends.

If you do not understand Hostess-PTSD, you may think any trepidation that a sixty-something woman has about having a few friends over for tea is simply a neurotic overreaction. You may think this, that is, right before you wonder if the family-buffet restaurant will be serving lobster this weekend.

For those of you who don't like seafood and are, therefore, still paying attention, I will explain:

Hostess-PTSD creates "flashbacks"—pictures in the mind, accompanied by swarms of angry butterflies in the stomach. My flashbacks include images of a creative Thanksgiving dinner with slow-tortured instead of slow-cooked game hens (crammed into a crock pot); a romantic dinner with cheese soup bubbling away in a dish advertised as safe to heat on the stovetop (don't try this at home); a major ant

14

infestation at my daughter's wedding dinner; berry cobbler presented at a potluck, which was berry pie before it slid off the oven rack. I could go on and on.

So, with my newly formed conviction that other people are not really watching my every move, I decided to face my fears of hostess-humiliation. I would fulfill my longing to use my fancy Christmas dishes. I would throw a Christmas tea party!

So I set the date, sent out invitations, and pictured what *I* would enjoy if *I* was a guest: food that is safe to eat, decorations with the proper holiday theme, and a hostess who is in control of her nervous breakdown.

"Are You Awake?" "Yes, Are You?"

As soon as I set the party date, I began waking at three in the morning for planning meetings with myself. I discovered special dishes on the Internet—complicated concoctions requiring blenders, choppers, and Martha Stewart. Nothing is too good for my friends.

Recognizing the name of some exotic ingredient in the gourmet aisle at the supermarket, I threw it into my basket so I wouldn't have to run to the store once I started cooking. I soon had a special area of my cupboard full of things like dandelion pesto, banana lentils, and daylily buds.

As the party date drew near, my husband sensed my preoccupation and called for a meeting. He turned the news down (during the commercial) and gave me his opinion that I was putting myself through something completely unnecessary. Revealing the slight irritation one feels when the words, "Can I help?" feel like a bottomless pit, he nobly suggested I simply take my friends out to lunch on our dime.

I explained again that being a hostess was something I'd wanted to do since I was a little girl and that certain unfortunate events had previously discouraged my natural party-giving nature.

Still, he fretted about me as I made lists and reminded him again and again of the day he had to be out of the house because *they* were coming.

When talking with my friends, I avoided mentioning all the preparations I was happily making. My friends are a collection of supermoms. They suffer extreme survivor guilt if anyone frets over something that will benefit them. They simply can't stand being the receiver instead of the giver.

For example, if I had mentioned that I'd be vacuuming the day before the party, someone would have showed up with her vacuum, determined to help me. If I had confided the menu to my indecisive friend, she would have second-guessed the advisability of serving cream cheese to dieters, the hazards of leaving certain foods out of the 'fridge too long, and the exact amount of alcohol that can safely be added to eggnog when people will be behind the wheel in three hours.

Better Safe than Sorry

At the last minute, I reread my exotic recipes and decided a tray of tea party sandwiches, picked up at the local supermarket; and pies, freshly baked out of their boxes, were really much more advisable for my down-to-earth buddies. I didn't want my friends to feel intimidated by my culinary skills. Instead of worrying about the food, I'd emphasize the fun of a party that stays on schedule.

When the big day arrived, I was on top of it. Every candle was lit, the music had repeated twice, and there was still an hour before the guests would arrive. Desperate to make time pass, I tested the camera by setting up the tripod and taking a picture of myself, waiting. I turned the heat under the spiced cider on and off. I blew out the candles and lit them again. I monitored the flow of traffic from my living room window, worrying about parking space.

Finally, there was a knock on the door. I basked in the obvious pleasure each arriving girlfriend got out of the whole shebang. Now I needed only to move them along.

Get the Show on the Road

It's difficult for people with Hostess-PTSD not to rush the dining a bit. I know it's not in the correct spirit to notice how much of each dish people put on their plates, how quickly they eat, and how much they leave. Yet I practically had to tie my hands behind my back to prevent myself from snatching their plates away so the party could go on. I wanted them to eat up and be done with it. I'd relaxed about food before, and that was when the cheese soup went all over the walls.

As for my own dining experience, I tasted nothing. My plate was filled and the food disappeared, but I have no memory of eating it. Later, after everyone had gone, I ate those leftover tea party sandwiches like a lumberjack.

Things almost got off schedule when everyone stopped to congratulate the winner of the cookie decorating contest, and I couldn't get her to hurry and open her prize and be duly surprised and delighted. Finally, I tapped a glass with a spoon and announced it was time for the Selfish-Santa gift exchange game.

When one recipient became tearful after her gift was "stolen" in the Selfish-Santa game, we agreed unanimously to rename the game "Satisfied-Santa" and keep the gifts we chose instead of trading them around. It's really a much more expedient way to exchange gifts anyway, and we needed to move on to the affirmation cards.

"Can I Come Home Now?"

We had just finished eating dessert, with my whole agenda complete, when the call came from my husband asking if he could come home now. The girls were talking fast and furiously, but I knew if I stood up and began putting away perishables, everyone would get the idea that it was time to clear out.

"How about forty-five minutes?" I whispered into the phone.

And in forty-five minutes I was glowing as I faced a sticky kitchen, burned-out candles, and a silent CD player I had forgotten about long before.

My Childish Dream

When I was a child, I had a little metal tea set. I set the table for my dolls and urged them to eat. I set up games and music and tried to help them have a good time. Unlike my current friends, my dolls never teased me about running my party like a drill sergeant, but they never really talked that much anyway.

When I was a young woman I tried to be a hostess; then the dog ate the truffles (which required an emergency trip to the vet); the apple pie (which I had hoped to serve warm) burned in the oven and set off the smoke alarm; and the invitations had a typo, which made everyone arrive two hours early. Sadly, I thought being a hostess was simply not for me.

Now I am retired and my party was called the best of the season. The Christmas tea party was my gift to my friends—and you know what? I pulled it off!

Seize the Day

Hey, woman, you too can pull off your childish dream, whatever it may be:

- Take piano lessons. You may feel old in a class of nine-year-olds at a recital, but just think—you're the only one who can pop a tranquilizer before it's your turn to play.

- Run/walk that marathon. We women over fifty finally know how to pace ourselves.

- Learn to play golf. No matter how you hit the ball, you can dress in the cutest outfits.

- Write that book. Having experienced an excellent self-publishing company, I can attest to the fact that you really can buy happiness.

- Learn to ride that horse. By now we know the secret of real power is not size but clever manipulation.

- Worry not about people who would call your efforts foolish—they are in the pudding line at the family-buffet restaurant.

- Ignore those who say, "You're going to do *what*?" Just put on your bifocals, read the directions, and do it now!

*Unlike my friends, my dolls never teased me about
running my party like a drill sergeant.*

Chapter 4

Live in the Past

Don't believe people who say you should not live in the past. When you allow your mind to drift back to bygone eras in your life, you can completely forget that your hands now look like your grandmother's hands and your feet now look like your *grandfather's* feet.

Join me, and I'll show you ways to make today more meaningful by remembering the past.

Let's begin with your photographs. Never mind when family members groan and say, "Clear the table! Grandma's taking out her albums again!" The ones who complain most about having their pictures taken and looking at family albums are usually the ones who elbow their way to the best spot for viewing.

The Way We Were

There are many uses for photo albums besides saving them for distribution after you're gone.

You can spark the old flame at anniversary time by leafing through pictures of the full-haired, bright-eyed, lusty young lovers you and your guy once were. There you are, camping and fishing and sitting on the tailgate with him; and there he is, dancing and going to church with you.

"Come look at how cute we were when we were young," you coax as he cuts his toenails.

"Be right there!" he answers, and you know he really *will* be right there, thanks to the training you've given him in the past.

Photo albums also come in handy for helping you recognize the beauty of your current age. As you look back at the hair, skin, and figure you were so critical of when you were young, you can see your current beauty from the perspective of twenty years from now.

Now that you are of retirement age, you probably have lots of photo albums, providing you ever got around to actually putting your pictures in albums. If not, you simply have boxes of pictures—*boxes and boxes* of pictures.

Another reason to remember the past is to prevent the creation of disappointing new memories. There are several ways to do this:

Birthday Rituals

If you are still waiting for other people to make you happy on your birthday, I highly recommend you finally take charge:

- Buy yourself the birthday gift you really want, and then, when you receive a bottle of mole remover, you can smile graciously.

- Get a manicure and pedicure; then you are ready for whatever life "hands" you as you spend the next year "on your toes."

- Eat out. If you are watching your portions, eat only half the slice of birthday cake in the restaurant, so you will deserve a piece of leftover cheesecake at home.

- Light candles as you thank all the people who stood beside you this year: family, friends, and the bedbug exterminator.

- Watch an old movie from childhood, such as *Black Beauty, Heidi,* or all the great episodes in the *Roy Rogers: Cowboy Classics* collection.

Birthdays and anniversaries only come once a year, but all year you can celebrate the past with frequent, inexpensive, and fabulous treasure hunts.

The Spirit of the Past

The spirit of the past is found in antique stores, flea markets, and yard sales. Old things that have survived rough treatment and the ravages of time are valuable and rare—like you and me!

Besides, for less money than it takes to stuff your grandkids with burgers, you can come home with bags full of things you remember from days gone by, such as milk bottles, crocheted doilies, and embroidered dish towels.

You will be the envy of all your friends when you display metal canisters with cherry decals like the ones your mother had, or a shovel with a hand-painted barn scene like the one your father had.

Sifting through dusty boxes provided by a sweaty guy with suspenders will start your heart pumping. Running your fingers over the titles of old books will remind you of childhood trips to the bookmobile with its delicious, musty smells. Poking through spider webs at estate sales will make you feel like Nancy Drew in the attic again.

It's true, secondhand goods were once considered low-class and shabby, but all the people racing down the street to get to yard sales these days demonstrate just how our society has evolved. As you clutter your present life with treasures from the past, you will evolve too.

And speaking of evolving, perhaps you would like to become a "collector."

"Olive, Help Me!"

I remember how my collection got started:

While walking in our horse corral years ago, I spotted a tiny rubber toy half-buried in the dirt. I was troubled that day. My career was driving me crazy. The trouble was not because of the work or the customers I served. No, I was caught up in the misery of a dysfunctional workplace.

How can I rise above petty politics and mind-numbing meetings and just do the work I love? I asked myself.

22

I reached down and picked up the little toy, buried in the dust by the horses' hooves. It was Olive Oyl!

In case you don't remember, Olive Oyl is the girl in the King Features Syndicate *Popeye* cartoons. She is known for skipping effortlessly across steel beams, miles above the hard ground. She sashays, untouched, through flaming buildings. She boldly stomps on gangplanks as she strides from ship to ship across treacherous seas. All the while, Olive sings a happy little tune with her eyes closed to the dangers around her.

Olive is sincere and continually forgives. She is always well dressed in black, red, and white. She keeps her firm footing with great big, substantial brown shoes. And she has a wash-and-wear hairstyle anyone would envy.

Even under the horses' hooves, the little figure was in her "Keep on truckin'" pose.

This is it, I said to myself. *Olive Oyl will show me the way.*

From that day on, I understood how grown people can be so delighted with their collections of bottle caps, stamps, toy trains, dolls, and all manner of childish, unnecessary, and totally cool stuff.

Collections serve many purposes close to the collectors' hearts:

- Collections remind us of the children living secretly in our aging bodies.

- Collections give us something to search for at flea markets besides our husbands.

- Collections make us smile the empty-headed smile of a small child with a mouthful of birthday cake, without the calories.

- Discovering an item for our collections gives us a chance to feel like winners, without even buying a lottery ticket.

- Showing off our collections to friends gives us an opportunity to prove to the world we don't care what they say about us when we're not around.

Try it! You, too, can collect something besides migraines, old driver's licenses, and bags of dried beans you'll never cook.

Oh, yes! Here's another important reason to live in the past: to write your memoir!

Do the "Write" Thing

Why would you hesitate to write your memoir? One, you don't know how; and two, you fear no one will ever read it anyway. We will deal with these writer's blocks together; but first, here are a few reasons why you simply *must* document your memories for yourselves and your families:

- If you don't write your stories, you will be compelled to tell them over and over at family dinners, to disinterested people in line at the grocery store, and to your busy doctor. Come now, this is not the way you want to live!

- Writing your stories will prevent you from forgetting them as your memory grows dim—and a memoir will give you something to read when you wonder where the years went.

- Without a memoir, when your days on earth are over and you are fading fast and mumbling away, it will not be the angels you are talking to. You will be making one last effort to tell about that teacher in sixth grade who changed your life—or the time the father you thought was born mute actually said he was proud of you.

Now, I will show you an easy way to write an interesting and entertaining memoir. Just complete the following sentences. Imagine you are talking to someone who is listening with great interest—*me*!

Okay, let's get started:

- My mother taught me …

- My father taught me …

- My grandmother taught me …

- My grandfather taught me …

- I learned in school ...

- I almost gave up when ...

- I was so proud when ...

- I believe love is ...

- The point of my life is ...

- To me, God is ...

- I give thanks for ...

- I hope for ...

- I want to be remembered for ...

You get the idea. Now that you've got a good start, you can think up more sentences to complete.

If you don't know how to use a computer, write in cursive. If you can't write in cursive, print. If you can't print fast enough, dictate into a tape recorder and get your grandchild to transcribe it.

Just keep on remembering.

If you start crying, you're on to something—blow your nose and continue. If you laugh, just keep writing away. Do at least a sentence a day, but don't rush the process. At last, you've started!

Eventually, you'll be ready to put it all together and become immortal.

That brings us to your second writer's block: "No one would want to read it anyway."

This argument is easy to dispute. Just ask yourself this question: If your mother or grandmother or great-grandmother had written a memoir by completing sentences in her own words, would you want to read it?

I rest my case.

Live in the Past

We reincarnate many times in life. You are not the same person you were when, as a little girl flying down the sidewalk, your roller skates came off your shoes. When you walked away from high school in your cap and gown, you walked into a new life. All the marriages, divorces, births, and deaths you lived through redefined you over and over.

To forget the past is much like a surprising "delete" when you haven't saved the document. Without your albums, rituals, collections, and memoir the world has a big blank where all your stories should be.

No one can tell your stories but you.

Go ahead; live a little—*in the past!*

*You can spark the old flame by leafing through pictures
of the lusty young lovers you once were.*

Chapter 5

Love Your Car

In lots of ways the challenges of driving build our characters by teaching us symbolic lessons of life:

- The art of safely passing those in our way

- The importance of heeding detour signs

- The ability to turn sharp corners in order to reach our destinations

- The advisability of not drifting into someone else's lane

- The value of sometimes shifting into overdrive

- The determination to develop a map before we take a journey

- The diligence to watch for landmarks as we travel along

- The desire to pay attention to what we're doing instead of drifting off into a debate with our passengers about whether or not that plastic gadget really gets the dead skin off our heels

North, South, East, What?

In addition to all these character-building lessons, our cars, like our adult children, also give us regular doses of humility. No matter how old we get, there are times our cars overpower us, let us down, or simply tease us into panic attacks.

Take the problem of getting lost. It is amazing that some well-directed people actually know the difference between north, south, east, and west simply by looking out the car window. Among these people are smug misogynists who work in convenience stores located off any confusing roadway. Their eyes glint with mischief, it seems, as they rattle off directions: "Go two blocks up, turn west, go east a mile or two, watch for the traffic light, turn left, and go north until you reach the freeway entrance."

Where Am I?

I once got lost at night while leading a carload of guests from the airport to my house. Somehow, the car lights confused me and I took a wrong turn. My cousin (a well-directed person), who was driving the other car, had been to my house only once before. When she saw me take the wrong turn she was puzzled, but she concluded I was picking up some snacks. She drove east and stayed on course to my front door.

I drove through the darkness of a neighboring town, 'round and 'round (duplicating a recurrent nightmare I have). I stopped a couple of times in dangerous territory to ask directions (got the north-south-east-west version). Finally, I cried out in desperation, "Why hast thou forsaken me?"

I made up with God after I accepted the miracle of a freeway entrance and was on my way again. By the time I reached my house hours later, my guests were considering calling Missing Persons.

I relate all this to justify the cost of my GPS. If you don't have a navigation system in your car, you must put it in your budget. Now my girlfriends and I can go to any darned garden tour we choose, no matter how ridiculous the directions in the flyer are. I can find my way to my sweet driveway from anywhere in the United States!

"Uh-Oh, What Does That Light Mean?"

Not only can our trusted vehicles lose us in space, there is also the issue of a sudden breakdown, or what *appears* to be a sudden breakdown.

By the time we reach retirement age we have learned that cars, relationships, health, and even our arches don't really break down all of a sudden. It just seems that way when we're having so much fun we ignore warning signs. Prevention is paramount if we want to avoid situations where we are standing pitifully on the side of the road, literally or figuratively.

Our relationships with our cars are similar to our relationships with our hair dryers: we know a breakdown can be a disaster, so we keep our eyes and ears open.

For example, we keep a close watch at the oil change place where young service people pretend to vacuum our cars after servicing them. We keep track of where our husband puts the little thingamajig tire tester, so he can find it when the tires are low. Likewise, we try to be patient and supportive when our husbands decide to check the oil level just as we are leaving for a party.

Furthermore, when we are behind the wheel our sensory perceptions are especially acute. Our noses perk up immediately if our grandchildren smuggle French fries into our car ashtrays or if our dogs bury chunks of dog-park debris under the floor mats.

Our ears are as finely tuned as our noses. We may not know anything about how the engine runs, but we can pick up a mechanical heart murmur as quickly as we pick up a veiled criticism from a friend.

After forty-five years of driving, we realize that our cars are simply extensions of our houses, which are extensions of our families, which are extensions of our hearts and souls.

Good Golly, Miss Molly!

All that said, there are times when we are driving along minding our own business and our perfectly good cars choke up, red lights flash, and we know we are in trouble.

We don't know what we should do first: feel angry at our husbands, blame the last oil changers who touched our cars, repeat words we would scold our adult kids for saying or, these days, simply pull over and get out our cell phones.

This recently happened to me. I was driving my beloved Miss Molly—a seventeen-year-old Cadillac—which I had proudly owned for thirteen years. Suddenly, the SUV next to me let out what sounded like a big belch of muffler trouble. I felt so sorry for the guy! Then he pulled away, but the belch continued. It was Miss Molly!

Naturally, when the mechanic said the blown transmission made fixing Miss Molly an exercise in bad judgment, I had to grieve yet another sign of the years flying by.

I loved Miss Molly, and loving my car made me amenable to hauling my friends around in spite of my fears of becoming lost or broken down. When passengers commented about Miss Molly being a "freeway floater" or a "boat," I laughed along, knowing they were just envious of the personality my car displayed for all the world to see.

In a parking lot, Miss Molly didn't blend in with all the other cars. Her tail stuck right out in our path, so we never had any trouble locating her, even when we were chatting so much we forgot to notice where we parked. I guess you could say Miss Molly was a "given" in my life.

Still, having loved and lost many times before, I knew immediately I must love again. I wondered, however, if I could really love a car without Miss Molly's style and grace.

Now I own another Cadillac, just the color of my favorite red lipstick. We have a new relationship, and I can't say I actually *love* my car yet, but I know it will come in time.

Adopt a Car!

A car should not be simply a means of transportation any more than a friend should be simply someone you run up your phone bill with. A car reflects what we're all about. Like us, age makes no difference at all. Hard miles only add to the charm. Each ding and dent only shows determination to keep going.

The important thing about our cars—and our lives—is to stand out a little. We don't want to blend in so completely we disappear. In some ways, our cars reveal whether we're in the drivers' seats as we travel along the road of life or if we're just along for the ride.

So, ladies, here's my advice: we must

- Rev up our motors

- Pull out into the traffic of life

- Fear no breakdowns

- Take the GPS

- Love our cars!

*When passengers called Miss Molly a "freeway
floater," I just laughed along.*

Chapter 6

KEEP TALKING (TO YOURSELF)

No one knows the importance of a heart-to-heart like a retired woman. Talking is our forte. We women *sense* things, like dogs feel the rumblings of an earthquake before anything really moves. What we sense, we want to talk about.

Now that we are retired and have plenty of time and energy, our sensors are working overtime. We want to offer understanding, compassion, and, of course, our hard-earned wisdom, through talking.

Why, then, do people so often run away, saying, "Nature calling!" when we want to talk with them?

I ask you this, dear reader, realizing you cannot possibly answer. This gives me the opportunity to go on talking and talking as I answer the question myself, which brings me to the point: *perhaps we talk too much.*

The experts say that when the speaker asks a question, she is probably just trying to get our attention. Never mind giving her an answer. Good listeners say, "What makes you ask that?" or some other frustratingly correct counter-question.

We've all heard this rule. We all know it's true. Yet, we all fudge on it all the time. Being the creative thinkers we are, we immediately have an answer to any question that may hang in the air. Then, having great big hearts prone to breaking over someone else's problem, we feel a frantic need to offer the solution as soon as possible. When we try to tuck the solution away for later—after she has had her turn to talk—it tickles the inside of our mouths until we are forced to spit it out. We all know how it feels to go away from a conversation realizing we interrupted, gave unsolicited advice, monopolized, and generally jumped on an innocent question like paparazzi on a nude celebrity.

When this happens, we must remind ourselves that she who blabs incessantly blabs alone, unless, perhaps, she is blabbing simultaneously with another retired woman. Even then, if we don't coach our own verbal output, we may find our friend excusing herself to give her dog a pedicure, paint a house, or have an affair with a fictional man.

So what are we talkers to do? How can we control our need to talk-talk-talk so we can be good listeners? Again, left alone with my question and eager to give a wise answer, I say we must keep talking—to ourselves!

There are many proven ways to do this.

Diaries, Journals, and Lists of Things to Do

Most of us had diaries when we were young. We especially loved the ones that had locks and keys, although we had a way of leaving our diaries unlocked on the living room coffee table, because we secretly hoped someone would be curious enough to read them. Although we pretended to protect our childhood diaries from almost everyone, nothing was more fun than reading them to our friends.

We wrote things in our diaries like, *If Mom would only realize—all the other girls shave their legs!* Such pronouncements were among our first efforts to stifle our impulses to scream at people who drove us crazy.

When we became teenagers, our diaries became much more personal, so we hid them in the bottom drawer under our frilly girl-things. We poured our hearts out in our diaries about boys: *I would like him so much if he just didn't have that wart on his left hand*; about other girls: *They don't like me, no matter what I do*; and about how we looked: *My shoes are so dorky!*

As we became young wives and mothers, our diaries became journals. A journal is a cross between a novel and a tirade. Grist for the mill of our journals included wondering what in the world our young husbands could possibly be thinking and how two-year-olds could be so powerful.

Even in our distressed states, we realized things change from day to day and we did not want to hurt someone we loved by venting about how we felt yesterday. So, we often made pacts with friends to secretly destroy our journals if we should suddenly die.

Now that we are in our "second adulthoods," we write things like letters we never send, contracts with ourselves, letters to the editor, and lists of things to do before we die. These are all great outlets for our gabby minds. We might even try to write a book!

Talking to Ourselves

Talking to ourselves through mumbling, exclaiming, and sometimes cursing softly is yet another way to vent some of the thoughts rattling around in our heads. By our ages, we are skillful at being our own best listeners; thus our excitement when we have our houses to ourselves.

Other places amenable to satisfying the need for self-talk are in the car while driving alone; at the mirror while putting on makeup; and, of course, in the tub while soaking.

Great insights are gained by talking to ourselves. Solutions to problems that were incubating during all the in-box/out-box chatter of a household become clear. Besides, it's a great way to remember why we came into a room.

Alas, although prattling to ourselves is productive and entertaining, we still can't wait until we can tell someone else all about whatever we come up with.

Talking in Our Sleep

It would be more accurate to say, "Talking to ourselves while we are *supposed* to be asleep."

Middle-of-the-night waking—so common with retired women—is usually blamed on hormones or, perhaps, the habit of trying to sleep face-up to avoid new facial creases from the pillow. Doctors will medicate us immediately if we call our nocturnal mental meanderings "worry." However, sleep medication helps very little, since then we must worry about where we might drive while asleep.

Actually, the sticky-notes in our brain are simply unfinished business from the day before. In the middle of the night, after we have had a good nap, we are ready to edit the opinions and decisions we were so sure of yesterday. It is time to "delete" and "restore" information on our mental computers.

For example, should we delete Pilates and restore yoga? Should we delete forty-five pounds and restore walking? Should we delete pedicures and restore massages? Should we delete resentment and restore forgiveness? Should we delete self-doubt and restore confidence? As I'm sure you know, our mental computer work goes on and on before we finally fall asleep again.

Although this nightly routine is not always comfortable, it is the best way to have an "Aha!" moment. Suddenly, we realize what was meant the day before by a weird and inappropriate glance, comment, or wisecrack. This insight is especially rewarding when *we* were the ones giving the glances, comments, or wisecracks!

If we welcome insomnia as a gift of retirement, we can hold unbelievably productive conversations with ourselves. Or we can just close our mental laptops, plug ourselves into our transistor radios, and listen to late-night jazz.

Talk-Therapy

There is much to be said for psychotherapy in later life. For one, it's fun. We have a captive audience. We have Medicare with which to pay. What's not to like?

The downside is that our therapists may not challenge us with give-and-take conversations. They may feel funny sharing their worries about spider veins and their husbands' resistance to (or insistence on) using Viagra. If all our therapists do is listen-listen-listen, we may begin to bore even ourselves.

If this happens, we must draw them out by repeatedly asking what they think. If therapists didn't love to talk about themselves, they wouldn't be therapists. They can't hold out forever. Soon they will be laughing at gravity with us.

Your Audience—To Have and to Hold

All our self-talk is as wasted as celery stored next to tapioca pudding if it doesn't make us better communicators. If we want to share our yak-yak-yak with real live human beings who are not snoring, we must follow the rules:

- We must yak no more than sixty seconds before observing our audiences. If our husbands, grandchildren, or friends are either glazed over, guzzling alcohol, or gone, we must say no more.

- We must expand our outlets for lively discussion. We must not lay all our neediness on our husbands and kids. They cannot act as sponges for our wordiness.

- If we never trusted other women, now is the time to get over it. Without the stimulation of female conversation, we become like pioneer women on the lonely, dusty prairie: eyeing our ice picks with way too much affection.

- We simply must exchange ideas with other women. This might mean joining women's groups, even if we swore at age fourteen we would never run for cheerleader again.

Wanted: Kindred Spirits

Many retired women have histories of being hurt by other girls. Therefore, trusting and forgiving women enough to seek them out may require courage and determination.

This is understandable. Competition is built into the female mind. We compete with cooking, cleaning, appearance, finances, and the condition of our fingernails. We batch up into cliques. We compare ourselves this way and that. We hurt each other with sarcasm. Anything that went wrong between us and our mothers circulates around our female friendships like smoke in a teepee; and what the interference of a man can do to a female friendship should not be written in print.

Still, there are many layers of friendship. Not every woman we enjoy has to be a best friend.

In fact, most women we meet will not become soul-sister confidantes, but there is someone for everyone. We must get out there and search for good-fitting women friends at least as earnestly as we search for good-fitting jeans.

Only other women know how it feels. How *what* feels? I have the answer!

Everything we need to talk about!

*We must search for good-fitting women friends at least
as earnestly as we search for good-fitting jeans.*

Chapter 7

DECORATE WITH "POP"

According to television experts, if we want our home décor to "pop," we must first rearrange the furniture. One day I decided to do this myself.

I mumbled that I really should wait until my husband or another strong helper arrived before I took a stab at moving the heavy stuff. However, a sense of urgency set in. Imagining a sudden-death experience and how embarrassed my friends would be for me if they had to gather in this tacky room for my memorial, I forged ahead with the heavy work.

Lifting first one side and then the other, I put sliders under the sofa and chairs and proceeded to push them around the living room. I pushed with my arms. I pushed with my hips. Finally, I lay down on the floor and pushed with my legs.

Following the lead of television experts, I began creating a conversation area: two cozy chairs and a little table for tea by a bright window. How nice.

I sat down a moment to think out of the box. Who said the dining table had to be in the dining room? I pulled, tugged, and threatened it into the living room. Now we had a reading nook in the dining area! Where would we eat? I'd think about that later.

What about the entertainment center? I rolled up my sleeves and transferred all the dusty books, videos, and overdue DVDs to the dining table. I unplugged the tangled mass of wires from the wall and slid the electronic devices onto a chair. Our old, heavy, analog television set objected at first, but finally fell facedown on a cushion. Then I wedged the oak entertainment center this way and that, until the dog ran out of the room with his tail between his legs. Sensing I was in danger, I decided to move on to another area of decorating.

I realized the lamps inherited from my parents had to go. Maybe my adult daughter would adopt them. I needed something unusual to replace the old-fashioned ceiling fan—perhaps something made of paper, straight from Taiwan.

By this time, my living room had the surprising look of a hairdo in a convertible. Perhaps I needed a break. I sat back and surveyed what I'd done. My back hurt. What did I do with the footstool? I had to face it: I really did need help, to put it all back where it had been before!

Fake Flowers and Other Home-Decorating Faux Pas

Yes, decorating our homes has become dangerous work. We watch the home and garden channel and suddenly our homes are dated, uninspired, or—heaven forbid—boring!

Redecorating begins with vague dissatisfaction and culminates in a driving compulsion to "stage" the entire house so anyone walking in the door would buy it, whether they're house-hunting or not.

The beds we make love in must have sheets with high thread counts. Wall art must inspire envy. Lighting must run on tracks. Fake houseplants are a disgrace. The horns-of-plenty on our dining tables must be replaced with absolutely *anything* else.

Heavy drapes must go. Window coverings must be light and airy, even if neighbors can see in. If we want privacy, we must go to the back of the house.

Look at those wires and cords in the entertainment center—we might as well have our bra straps showing! In fact, entertainment centers holding all our DVDs and other junk are passé. Likewise, the stuffed animals lined up along the back of our sofas ... they may fill us with happiness, but they are the stuff of home-decorating humiliation.

Our homes need a color theme. One wall in every room should be a surprising color, preferably reflecting the occupants' personalities:

blue for water lovers, green for gardeners, yellow for … your guess is as good as mine!

Furniture will bring bad luck if it is not arranged with feng shui. We must always face looking outward.

There should be no clutter. If family pictures must be displayed, they should be arranged on our walls in creative frames, but never, ever, if the goal is to sell the house. In that case everything personal must go. No one wants our worn-out sentiments.

When Our Homes Were Just Where We Lived

Back in the day when we retired women were growing up, home decorating had a different set of rules. First and foremost, it was important *not* to be different from the neighbors. No one wanted to be considered "eccentric." From there, the rules were quite simple:

- Drapes were closed at night, so we wouldn't "live in a goldfish bowl."

- The furniture sat in one position from the day it was delivered. Why move it?

- A large picture with a gold frame hung over the sofa. The subjects varied from women in Victorian garb to ocean scenes.

- End tables with "never-mar" tops were placed on either side of the sofa. These tables held matching lamps with cone-shaped bases and rather dusty lampshades with lace trim.

- A matching coffee table was placed exactly in front of the sofa with a black ceramic panther on one end and an ashtray on the other.

- Having wall-to-wall carpet was a way of keeping up with the Joneses. It was usually long shag of a very cheerful color like harvest gold or lime green.

- Hanging on the wall were "whatnot" shelves, holding collections of salt and pepper shakers, spoons, or thimbles— all of which provided surefire Mother's Day ideas.

- The kitchen floor was linoleum and proud of it. It worked well for a game of jacks.

- The chrome dinette set almost always had a small rip on at least one of the plastic chairs.

- Fake fruit in a horn-of-plenty acted as a centerpiece and a conversation starter: "That fruit sure looks real!" people would say.

- The bathroom tile was turquoise. The tub and shower were cleaned by children forbidden to go out and play until the chores were done.

Buy New Throw Pillows

But this is today, right? Our mothers did not have stores with such an array of inexpensive and charming stuff for our homes. Who can resist bamboo doormats with leopard trim, food choppers in bright colors, vases made of cut glass, dishes with inlaid diamonds?

We retired women go to the home décor stores ("just to look") and forget all about fights with our husbands, lost friendships, numbers on the scale, and even numbers on the blood-pressure monitor.

We know our eyes are as glazed as the eyes of all the other women wedging their carts through narrow aisles lined with treasures. We laugh at ourselves as we delight in candleholders made of mirrors, aprons with sarcastic slogans, and scrub brushes that look like dolls with faces and spiky hair.

When we get to the cashier, we can't believe the "reasonable" total of our purchases. Then, when we get home, we are only slightly sheepish thinking about what our parents would say as we carry our plastic bags into the house.

Once inside our homes, we decorate and decorate and decorate! It's fun!

Call Us "Eclectic"

We retired women love to make our home décor "pop" with our mix of modern and old-fashioned stuff, even if no one would want to buy our cluttered houses.

Let the experts snicker; some things will decorate our homes as long as we are drawing breath, and we have our reasons:

- Tablecloths, crocheted by our mothers, because they give us comfort.

- Plaster-of-paris handprints, because they remind us of grandchildren on duty somewhere in a dangerous part of the world.

- Worn sofas, because they are perfect for snuggling with lovable dogs on cold winter nights.

- Our husbands' contributions, like Indian arrowheads framed and hung on the wall, because they give him something to show off during awkward silences when people are visiting.

That Chair Is Just for Looks

Some of us retired women hire professional decorators, so if our friends don't like the effect, we can blame someone else. Some of us insist on decorating our homes from the ground up, even doing our own painting and wallpapering, which often results in re-painting and re-wallpapering. Some of us just dream of what a great decorating job we will do, "as soon as we get around to it."

Some of us move our furniture so often we keep chiropractors in business. Some of us solve the whole decorating dilemma by no longer watching the home and garden channels.

All of us retired women realize by now that whatever we decide to do so our home décor can "pop," we must not move our overstuffed chairs away from our entertainment centers. We need them there so we can sleep through our favorite television programs.

*I wedged the entertainment center this way and
that until I realized I was in danger.*

Chapter 8

Direct the Eastside

One of the great illusions of retirement is that we are going out of business. Actually, retirement is big business and, as usual, keeping it all going falls to the brave, the swift, and the well-fed—in other words, us retired women!

My husband and I like to say he is the westside director and I am the eastside director. This means he fills the grocery cart with surprising and unfamiliar items, and I find a place in the kitchen to store them. Likewise, he checks the oil in the cars and I sprinkle sand on the oil spots. He fills the refrigerator with leftovers, and I throw them out. You get it.

Anyway, we women never really retire from being eastside directors. If we wrote job applications for the position of eastside director of retirement, we would still say, as we did in our youthful resumes, that we want to fulfill our aptitudes, skills, and talents. Directing the eastside gives us every opportunity to fulfill our aptitudes (by controlling what goes on), our skills (by putting things in order before they bury us), and our talents (to make simple things complicated.)

The Infrastructure of Retirement

In order to direct the eastside adequately, it is imperative that we have decent work environments. While retired women of yore needed a room with a view, retired women these days need a home office with a view of our file cabinets.

When I opened my retirement home office, my husband was amazed that I needed three full-size file cabinets.

"You're retired," he said. "What are you going to put in all these file cabinets—burial instructions?"

Men don't understand why file cabinets are a retired woman's best friend, just as they don't understand why diamonds are a girl's best friend. But they haul the file cabinets into the house anyway—just happy the office supply store doesn't sell jewelry.

It doesn't matter if our file cabinets are metal or fancy-furniture oak. The important thing is that we accept them as home décor pieces, even if our home office takes over the formal living room.

The business of retirement roughly falls into three categories: personal business, other people's business, and rigmarole, each of which requires at least one full-size file cabinet.

Personal Business

Our personal business file cabinets hold files that organize important things like

- Birthdays of friends, relatives, friends' and relatives' kids, their kids' kids, and so on.

- Lists of gifts given, to be given, received and kept, donated to charity, and actual gifts stored in the file cabinet for re-gifting.

- Mail order catalogs to be studied; mail orders never sent because of expensive shipping; mail orders sent regardless of expensive shipping; pending requests for replacement or refunds on defective merchandise; and copies of angry, "What a gyp!" letters sent to mail order catalogs.

- Tempting brochures collected from home shows, holding out hope that, even though retired and poor, we may someday get one of those whole-house fans or little round skylights.

- Stacks of "Last Chance! Renew Now!" magazine subscription notices—received as part of a conspiracy to frighten us into renewing our subscriptions into the next century.

- Physical fitness brochures depicting the miracles of Pilates, yoga, tai chi, spinning on a stationary bike, and other revolutionary ways to stay young that we will never actually stick to. Also found in this drawer are business cards and flyers for manicurists, pedicurists, and even a massage therapist reputed to perform miracles on problematic areas like shoulders, hips, and muffin-bellies.

- Invitations to lectures on ten ways to do things: ten ways to find happiness, to become ageless, even ten ways to find an honest financial advisor.

- And finally, brochures for classes on "mindfulness," which teach deep relaxation as a result of talking to a raisin.

One whole drawer of our personal file cabinet is filled with materials from all the board of directors' groups we have joined.

At first we attend board meetings as courtesies to washed-up board members pleading for replacements. We have no intention of joining the boards, much less becoming officers. We attend just to stop the whining.

When does "No" become "Well, okay"? It happens so gradually—similar to the slow but relentless emergence of those brown spots on our hands.

Finally, we have the section of our personal filing systems bulging with travel guides; these are not only for trips friends took that we envied, but also for guided outdoor adventures for couples—hunting, fishing, and camping—that our husbands brought home for us to "look over."(These are yellow with age.)

Other People's Business

Now that we are retired, our noses are often welcome in other people's business. This is especially true if at some point in our lives we successfully sobbed our way through learning how to use a computer.

Once friends discover we know how to "Google," they are quick to spread the news. Thus, we must have a cabinet holding files full of research other people will soon "drop by" to pick up.

Waiting for pickup any day now:

- Online research on senior belly-dancing techniques and lessons.

- Information from websites for angel advocates.

- Recipes for tea party sandwiches, Mexican salads, and various ways to spike calcium drinks.

- Successful honeymoon techniques for the late-in-life bride and groom.

- Tips on tipping when out to lunch with friends.

- How-to files, which are especially numerous:

  - How to brew medicinal tea from overgrown bamboo shoots and other invasive plants.

  - How to perform on the piano while playing with only two fingers.

  - How to downsize without getting rid of anything.

  - How to avoid landing in a nursing home by volunteering in one.

  - How to iron out facial wrinkles.

  - How to decorate for every season with one string of lights.

  - How to grandparent on a budget.

  - How to convince your adult children that you know what you're doing.

Larger items for the other people's business file cabinet include things like:

- Doggy cleanup bags for the friend who brings her nervous little pooch to visit.

- Grown-up diapers for the friend who springs a leak while laughing.

- Bedroom books and videos—best hidden from visiting grandchildren.

- Cookies to serve to friends who drop in—best hidden from husbands.

All of these bring us to the third file cabinet my husband managed to place in the home office after adding yet another chip to the door frame with the dolly.

Rigmarole

"Why," my husband asks, "do you have to file away rigmarole?"

If he understood what "rigmarole" is, he wouldn't need to ask. Rigmarole is all the stuff that ends up lost just when we need it the most. Therefore, it is important that we not tell our husbands what rigmarole is, so they won't grab our rigmarole when they have lost their own rigmarole. This includes:

- Hammers, drills, and other tools for suddenly urgent projects, such as installing twenty hooks upon which to hang twenty baseball caps, which multiply on the closet floor like credit card charges at Christmastime.

- Package tape for mailing packages to kids who will never write thank-you notes.

- Batteries of all sizes to breathe new life into our clocks, calculators, and foot massagers. (We also store things like actual foot massagers just so we'll know where they are when the people who gave them to us for Christmas come to visit.)

- Fabric grocery bags picked up at various stores for ninety-nine cents and always in the drawer—never at the grocery counter—when needed.

- Yard sale treasures that are no longer cute and soon must go.

The View from Here

So, ladies, we might as well enjoy our home offices, because they are here to stay. When we sit at our desks and view our file cabinets, we know we still have the business of life under control.

We may not earn money anymore, but we are still valuable. After all, we are the eastside directors!

"Why," my husband asks, "do you have to file away rigmarole?"

Chapter 9

GET A DOG (OR NOT!)

For some retired women, deciding whether or not to include a dog in their retirement paradigm is a no-brainer. "Of course," they say, "I *must* have a dog!"

Other women laugh at the idea. "No way," they say. "The sliding glass door is clean for the first time in years!"

The third group, in which I used to be, gets stuck in, "Should I, or shouldn't I?"

Surrounded by pamphlets warning that getting a dog is a commitment that would carry me into the next decade, I freaked out. At this point, my decades are not to be trifled with. What if I got a dog and changed my mind? On the other hand, what if I didn't get a dog and regretted it someday in the nursing home?

My indecision was not new. It was the same when I was young, only then my dilemmas involved whether to have a baby or go back to college, quit a boring job or join a bowling league, leave a guy or eat a gallon of ice cream. (I had the baby *and* went to college, quit the job *and* joined the league, left the guy *and* ate the ice cream!)

Then, as I was deciding about getting a dog, after a restless night with feelings as scattered as my bed covers, I knew there was only one thing to do. I had to call for a summit meeting with my retired girlfriends. They would help me sort out all the pros and cons.

Phone-Tree

They arrived in a flurry, armed with laptops and chocolate. There are few things that mobilize the creative energy of women like a true dilemma. Passions ran high and we all talked at once. Little by little, our list of pros and cons was hammered out:

Pro:

Dogs give us something warm to take care of. A bag of flaxseed warmed in the microwave just won't do it.

Con:

Think again. We retired women have taken care of others all our lives. Now that we are retired, we resign from caretaking. We want to play with friends; travel; and experiment with hobbies like painting, making music, and wearing clanking jewelry. It's high time for a little "me-me-me."

Pro:

But dogs keep us grounded in the true values of a good life. They prevent us from becoming so fixated on our own reflections in our magnifying mirrors that we are never happy, no matter how much cosmetic work we have done.

Con:

Having a dog is a lifestyle. Dog ownership means hesitating to go to a three-hour movie or any activity that leaves the poor thing trapped inside, dreaming of a tree upon which to lift his leg. When a dog is our home's official greeter, instead of "Welcome!" we must begin every visit with, "Down! Down!"; and even a tiny dog can impact the bedroom with a serious case of "canine interruptus."

Pro:

For all they give us, dogs ask very little: to live in the house near those they love, to be fed on schedule, to know the rules, and to be set free a little while every day—basic needs we all have. Actually, dogs allow us to write their job descriptions. No longer required to guard the ranch and chase beef and mutton around, now they earn their keep by kissing away our loneliness and reminding us to live in the moment.

Con:

Just the thought of getting a puppy or rescuing an abandoned dog can make a retired woman weary. True, when we see a cute puppy or beautiful canine companion, we are tempted. But if we make the commitment we will fulfill it, even at the expense of commitments we make to ourselves. Been there, done that.

Pro:

But dogs pull us away from our computers and out to the walking trails. Their pleading eyes make us laugh as they remind us of certain men we once dated. Their wagging tails teach us to bestow happiness with just a touch. Their willingness to beg and otherwise manipulate us keeps our boundaries strong. They instill balance in our lives: a bit of structure, a bit of discipline, a bit of delayed gratification, and a healthy amount of denial.

Con:

Dogs are big business. They require drawers of files and equipment. There are files for the groomer, vet, kennel club, licensing, and the dog park rules. That's not all. There are files for dog food coupons, excellent handmade doggie sweaters, dependable pet-sitters, and medication regimens and supplies. Don't forget the file holding names and addresses of potential dog-walking buddies.

In my case, storing all the necessary dog-owner files and records will also mean watching my husband bang his way into my home office with yet another file cabinet.

Pro:

Dogs give us an excuse to leave a boring party. They keep us warm on cold winter television-viewing nights. When we have an upsetting conflict with a human, they understand. They, too, have been hurt by mean words or an impatient look. After all is said and done, dogs are role models for forgiveness.

When Do We Adjourn?

At some point, the girls and I reached the conclusion that the pros and cons we really needed to study were not about dogs at all. The real problem was the potential dog owner: in this case, *me*!

If I got a dog, would I be able to go on a cruise without feeling so guilty I spent all my time on the phone saying things like, "Whose baby are you?" Can I be firm and say, "No, you're too fat for a cookie," without going on a cookie binge myself? Would I be willing to tell my dog, "You can hold it," before heading out for a long shopping spree?

My consultants and I had worked hard. Our lipstick was long gone and the chocolate was a memory; but we all agreed we were getting very close to something—happy hour, perhaps, or the *Dr. Phil* show, or a need to congregate in the hot tub.

We disbanded for the day, concluding I had to "incubate" the dilemma. Answers would come when the time was right.

He Shall Be Called "Bolt" (as in "Bolt of Lightning")

A few days later, I was driving along a quiet road with my girlfriends, still mired in indecision about whether or not to get a dog. Suddenly, a dog wandered in front of my car. I slowed to a stop and the dog just sat there.

"That's it!" our angel advocate joyfully declared. "It's a sign! There are no accidents!"

The dog looked nothing like my vision. Instead of small and furry, it was lanky and hairless.

"I don't know …" I murmured.

"No, really!" our storyteller jumped in. "This is why you haven't been able to decide. This dog was *waiting* in your future!"

Swept away by the romance of it all, I slowly stepped out of the car.

"*Here boy*," I coaxed, snapping my fingers cautiously.

The dog looked at me like I was crazy. He trotted away, glancing warily over his bony shoulder.

"Get out your cell phone and call the dogcatcher!" someone suggested. "After he's safely in the pound, we'll all go get him."

By then we were as giddy as we would be on a scale registering ten pounds light.

Can You Babysit the Dog?

Major life changes always follow a story line. By the time we're retired, we could write novels about how we came to be where we are right now in our lives. It all makes sense when you look back on it. The doggie dilemma was just another chapter in my quest for meaning.

On the way home we shared an epiphany: The most important "pro" of getting a dog would be the fun I could have sharing her with my retired women friends. A dog could open up all kinds of new activities for our gang. We could plan whole outings around going to dog shows, dog craft fairs, dog-friendly restaurants, and doggy bakeries.

My friends swore they would even sample sweet potato dog treats with my dog—if he asked them nicely.

Dogs pull us away from our computers and out to the walking trails.

Chapter 10

SHHH! X-RATED!

Sexual talk among retired women usually erupts as a surprise—perhaps while sharing tiny bites of heavenly crème brûlée with separate spoons.

"Is it true we have a finite number of orgasms in our lives?" someone muses, as she slowly draws her spoon from her mouth.

"Funny you should mention that," another says with a strange smile. "Just the other day I was wondering the same thing."

"Finite number of what?" a third girlfriend chimes in.

Spoons are suspended in midair. We all look at her. Is she serious? Could this sister be in need of last-minute sex education?

"Or-ga-sms," someone says in a loud whisper. "You know, the 'big-o'; *multiple ones*, even."

"I thought orgasms were a Freudian myth," admits our sweet late-bloomer.

"The myth is 'vaginal' orgasms," our wise woman says patiently. "You know, that you should have a big-o by remote control."

Everyone sits silently while a couple comes within earshot of our table on their way to the door.

"I believed in that myth for years and years," a voice chimes in as soon as they've passed. "Finally, I read a book and it changed my life."

"Books changed my life too," another admits with a smile. "But it wasn't Freud. They were books I found under my son's bed."

"You're kidding! You read 'smut'? How could you? It's so demeaning to women. Besides, how romantic is that? Isn't your lover enough?"

"Not necessarily," the reader defends. "You know, fantasy is a great avenue to the big-o. It's perfectly okay. It's harmless. And, yes, it's definitely smut."

"I never found a really good lover in all the times I've been married," says one, as she accepts the pretty young server's offer of another cup of coffee.

"Me either," the server says with a giggle. She removes our crème brûlée dish—which is practically licked clean. "Should I give up hope?" the server asks.

"The hope lies in yourself, honey," our wise woman decrees in a husky whisper. "We must be responsible for our own big-o's. How can a guy know what we need? The sad thing is they believe all the myths too. If they try too hard, it can result in real overkill."

"I can't believe we're discussing this!" says our shyest pal, with great indignation. "Where is all this leading?"

"To our bedrooms with our vibrators?" someone says, before she can stop herself.

The group's shriek is too loud. People at other tables glance over, see the age of our group, and go back to eating, unperturbed.

"So," our late-bloomer speaks up again, "I think maybe I've missed something. I was married for over forty years, and I felt great about sex because I never said no. I wondered about the big-o, but I figured it was just a myth—like all the other myths about marriage."

For a moment the group is quiet to the point of sadness.

"What other myths?" one of us has the presence of mind to ask.

"Oh, you know, like those things they say about size. Having never slept with any other man, I really wouldn't know. But I'm curious. Do you think he'll mind my size—that I'm not as thin as I used to be?"

"That's what she thinks they mean by 'size'?" someone whispers.

"What else would they mean?" our innocent friend asks.

"Let's drop that subject," someone suggests. "Let's talk about love."

"What about love?" the questioner quickly asks. "Does love make a difference if you want a big-o?"

"You betcha!"

"All the difference in the world!"

"Absolutely!"

"Without a doubt!"

"So," she goes on, "you *can't* have a big-o if you're not in love?"

Knees cross and uncross. Eyes peer over coffee cups.

"Dear, I'll tell you as I told my granddaughter," speaks the wise woman in the corner, "the big-o is sex. Sex is part of us from day one. You can be happy as can be with your overall life—but it's just like a smile with one tooth missing if you don't have sex. Yet, at the same time, love is not sex and sex is not love. Draw your own conclusions."

Our facts-of-life student looks as confused as I'm sure the granddaughter did.

"Well," our student finally resumes, "the reason I ask is, there's this gentleman who's come to call a few times. I feel really different with him: *excited*, I guess you'd say. I will hardly let him kiss me: it's too scary, but I want him to, I really do. I can't say I really *love* him, not like I loved my husband; but I'm just wondering if, maybe, it's not too late for me to have—you know—a big-o!"

"You can learn how!"

"I've got a book somewhere around the house!"

"Practice makes perfect!"

"It's never too late!"

"But about the size thing," she continues in spite of the blush traveling down her shirt collar, "I'm a little self-conscious about—*my weight*. I mean, he's not trim either. But do you think my weight will turn him off?"

"Another myth!" declares our wise woman. "Actually, research says overweight people are sexier than skinny ones. It's an appetite thing. When people have a great appetite for food, they also have a great appetite for all of life's pleasures. I say go for it!"

"I won't become a nympho, will I?"

"Hopefully," someone says, trying to be funny.

"How would you define a 'nympho' anyway?" our deep thinker asks.

"Well," says our student, "I once heard of a woman and a donkey. I don't know exactly what they did, but I figure if it had anything to do with sex she must be a nympho."

"Actually," our wise woman answers with great gravity in her voice, "I think pole dancers and the donkey woman and other exotic sexual beings probably enjoy sex much less than the rest of us. To them it's just business. That doesn't sound like any fun at all."

"Well," pipes up a longtime wife, "I believe if you use it you won't lose it. That's no myth."

The group looks at her with admiration.

"I'm not sure that's true for everyone," another says with a raised eyebrow. "But even if *certain* unfortunate things happen, a marriage can still rock with some really hot memories."

Heads nod in somber agreement. Someone wipes away a tear.

"All I know is," the shy one pipes up, "I'm glad I have those memories."

A dreamy mood settles over the group.

The table quiets down. It's rare that retired women don't compete for the floor. When that happens, watch out.

"Let's share another crème brûlée!" someone says suddenly.

"I second that!" another joins in.

"I can never get too much!" a third woman says to the giggling hostess.

Note: All names, ages, marital statuses, sexual functioning, and lifetime number of big-o's are strictly confidential. Only our lube-tubes know for sure!

Only our lube-tubes know for sure!

Chapter 11

Downsize Your Troubles

There comes a day when you look at your life and simply say, "I don't want to do this anymore." Suddenly you want to jump the fence, turn over a new leaf, make a new plan.

So you retire.

At first you wake up in the morning, see your name tag there on the dresser by your purse, and you believe you are footloose and fancy-free. Eventually, though, you remember: now that you're retired, you have no excuse for ignoring the duties you took on in exchange for retirement. You are now the gardener and housekeeper. You said, when the retirement plans were made, it would be your dream come true to finally get your corner of the world in some kind of order.

Be Careful What You Wish For ...

Each morning, now that you are retired, you leisurely drink your coffee and look out your kitchen window at something you hardly noticed before: a crop of oleander marching with the strength of an army from your side of the fence to the sliding glass door of your neighbor's house. It really needs to be trimmed! There's no use hoping your husband will look out the window, take pity on you, and massacre the oleander with a chain saw. He is not retired.

If you look out another window, you see all the leaves the paid gardener blows from hidden corners of the yard to the patio and sidewalks of your home. He is a pretend gardener. He loves the sound of his own blower, and he never removes his earplugs when you scream at him.

Then there are the weeds. When you went to work each day, you could avert your eyes from the flat weeds, the tall weeds, the weeds with stickers, and the weeds disguised as flowers. Since you retired, you've had time to gain a new respect for the weeds. You now realize they are so full of life, determination, and resilience, inspirational poems could be written about them.

Like everyone says, now you are retired and you have "nothing but time." It's just you and the weeds, together, with nothing but time.

You Might Get It!

Aside from the routine duties of yard care, there are bigger challenges awaiting you out there on your "property."

Now that you "no longer work," there is no excuse for avoiding the *shed,* that bulging place of darkness in the back of the yard where black widow spiders build condos under castaway lawn furniture, broken shovels, forgotten flowerpots, and bags of shredded bark.

You could seclude yourself indoors, but don't kid yourself; there's no safety inside your house either.

One of the conditions of retirement was that you would become the housekeeper again; so, you are now owned by a home with ten rooms to vacuum, two toilets to clean, and an acre of dust to chase around with one of those magnetic mops that hold out so much hope in television commercials.

In your working days you had a cleaning service. You arrived home from work full of happy anticipation. The "little fairies" had been there—and everything was magically clean. How easy you thought it would be to exchange earning money for the "light" duties of housekeeping. Now you remember why, when you were a teenager, your mother threw water on you to wake you up on Saturday mornings: it was housecleaning day!

Go Ahead! Throw Water on Me!

Having become aware of what you traded your career for, you wake in the morning with your head under the covers and a sense of dread creeping into you. You worked hard for retirement. You saved your money. You dreamed of freedom. You assured everyone, most importantly yourself, retirement would be the answer to your quest for contentment.

You fight it, you really do; but your mind screams at you until you have to listen. The words are very clear, and this time the message is about your retired life:

I don't want to do this anymore!

Okay. I admit it. I'm not talking about you. I'm talking about what happened to *me*. Or maybe, what happens to retired women everywhere. Maybe I'm talking about what happens to *us*.

There are lists of things we want to do when we finally retire: have lunch with friends, read for pleasure, spend time with the grandkids, walk off our stress, write that book, and resume piano lessons suspended at age nine.

How is it possible to live the dream, though, with the literal "trappings" of a big house and yard?

Sit Down, Darling

When I told my husband I needed to "have a talk," he blanched.

"What's up?" he asked. "Don't tell me you want to go back to work!"

"Just the opposite …" I began. "I want to retire even more. I want to sell the house and move into a mobile home community like the one my friend Laura lives in. I want to downsize."

"You want to live in a trailer park?" He looked at me the very way he looked at me when I told him, thirty years ago, that he and I were getting married.

"It's not called a trailer park anymore," I said with conviction. "They are 'mobile homes' now. They're cute little places with a simple lifestyle. It will be a whole new paradigm."

"I've seen Laura's place," he said with folded arms. "If there's a license plate on the back, it's a trailer!"

"Think about it," I coaxed. "When we wake up Saturday mornings, instead of deciding if we will spend the day hacking down oleander or staining the deck, we can decide what yard sales to go to or … maybe … *you know.*"

He looked at me with squinty eyes, and I knew I had him.

"Let me see if I get this straight," he said. "You wake up on one of your first free days in retirement, and you want to sell the farm, downsize to a whole new lifestyle, and basically go back to how we lived in our college days. Just like that, right?"

I hesitated. Was it really that simple?

"That's it," I agreed. "I want to live like we did in our college days, but without the need to prove ourselves and without the financial worry. Now, that's retirement!"

Back Under the Covers

I admit, the thought of downsizing your life can be as exhausting as the thought of continuing as it is. There's the task of readying a house for sale, a house with twenty-plus years' worth of this-and-that tucked away in hidden places.

There's the attic, with all the holiday decorations you never use anymore; the boxes of fat clothes and skinny clothes; and the boxes of who-knows-what, sprinkled with suspicious tufts of fiberglass insulation, shredded paper, and mouse droppings.

There's the garage, with the holiday decorations you actually do use; and the tools … *oh, so many tools!* There are the bicycles the grandkids might want to ride someday if the tires aren't flat. In case the tires are flat, there are several tire pumps, none of which will work on the newfangled tire stems anyway.

There's the sheet of plywood just right for a science project for kids now grown and on their own for twenty years. There's the stuff you're storing for your grandson in the army. There are cleaning products for everything from removing pitch from your windshield to getting rust out of a wheelbarrow.

Then there's the aforementioned "shed"—a cross between a garden shed and a hideaway for all manner of metal, steel, rubber, and wooden things that only men know the name of or the possible use for. It's a frightening place—off-limits to children, dogs, and anyone who might be attracted to taking advantage of a homeowner's insurance policy.

The household closets are no better. There are stacks of linens, lost in a closet world of "too good to throw away," and "not good enough to give away." There are miscellaneous toys from yard sales and the dollar store; and treasures stored on odd shelves long ago, so the grandkids could have "their own space." These areas are frozen in time by the phrase "Don't get rid of that," uttered by teenage grandkids now driving off in cars.

Only by filling piles of cardboard boxes are we able to downsize our house. We sort, haul, laugh, and cry. Downsizing goes on and on; and it feels good.

When we think the house is finally ready to put on the market, we develop a relationship with a realtor who breaks the news to us that our house is still a mess. We paint. We refurbish. We wonder if the day will ever come when we can *really* retire.

Downsizing, for Real

Here's the deal. When you live in a smaller space, you cannot add anything without getting rid of something; that means clothes, tools, cleaning supplies, yard sale trinkets, the whole Marianne.

You cannot offer to take your grandchild in when he or she needs to sit around and "sort things out." You cannot have a dog that yaps all night. You cannot impress friends with how affluent you are. You cannot host a wedding at your home.

You can still garden, but it's what I call "lady gardening." That is, you buy a pansy and plant the pansy. You water the pansy and talk to the pansy. You don't draw a diagram on graph paper for your new "outdoor living space."

In our mobile home community, we have a utility yard. For a nominal extra fee, my husband can rent two or three spaces large enough for his fishing boat, our RV, and his all-terrain vehicle.

No, he cannot store his outdoor equipment next to our house; but he can go fishing without neglecting a fence repair. He can ride up and down hills, or whatever guys do on their ATV machines, without worrying about the broken lawn mower. Furthermore, we can take camping trips in our RV without any concern about someone camping out in our house while we're gone.

Our shed is now a sacred place. Nothing goes in unless something comes out. Okay, I admit we still have the cleaning product that removes pitch from the windshield.

Downsizing to mobile-home living is not right for everyone, but it's just right for us. We cannot remember a time of life when we have felt so relaxed, so "together," or so free.

I hope you wake up after retirement, stretch your arms (not too hard; muscles don't snap back so quickly nowadays), and say, "This is living!"

But if you should wake up and want to put your head back under the covers, perhaps it's time to have a talk with yourself about what is really important to you these days.

There are lots of ways to live, and sometimes less is much, much more!

"I've seen Laura's place," he said with folded arms. "If there's a license plate on the back, it's a trailer!"

Chapter 12

Group Hug!

My retired girlfriends and I sometimes need an encounter group. True, we are happy, relaxed, and fulfilled. Yet, we are worried. We need to deal with something that bums us out each time we look in a mirror: *aging.*

If you'll remember, encounter groups were big in the seventies. They were a special place and time to be real. Everyone's goal was to gain self-awareness and get past mental blocks. We tried to help each other look for "scripts": ways of thinking and reacting that didn't work for us. We did it by being authentic and listening with a "third ear." If we shared enough of our secret thoughts and emotions in our encounter groups, we would watch each other grow from "dysfunctional, wounded children" to "functional adults" right before our eyes. It was so "rad"!

Nowadays, we girls will be sitting around sipping a sweet wine, discussing something like the pros and cons of using magnifying mirrors to put on our makeup, when our talk will suddenly become meaningful.

"Hey," one of the ladies pipes up, "remember our all-women sex-therapy groups in the seventies? We looked into mirrors to see our cervixes for the first time! We resented that doctors saw everything with a bright light, while we had never actually seen our secret gardens. It was powerful!"

"Those were the days," another says. "I went to a 'her-story' class in college. You know, 'her-story' rather than 'his-story.' It changed my life.

We talked about great women no one had ever heard of, because men wrote history. We burned our bras and chanted the motto, 'Step out of his shadow into the sunlight of liberty!'"

"I remember those women's lib groups," the gal in the corner says. "Once I went to lunch with no makeup. Not even my eyebrows!"

"I went to a Lesbian dance when I was young. All the female energy was amazing. I loved it, but the only girls I was attracted to looked like guys."

"What I remember is going from the diaphragm to birth control pills. I was a wild flower child. How cool was that?"

Silence.

"I remember the day I could look in the mirror and not think one thought about gray hair or wrinkles."

"I just wish I had my face back. The work I had done was okay, but I still don't recognize myself."

"I thought I would be a flower child forever. Time sure flies."

A general sense of melancholy sets in.

"Ladies," I say, regressing back to the sappy "caretaker" voice I was confronted about in my first encounter group, circa 1972, "remember, this doesn't feel good, but it's all part of the process. Feeling sad about what we're losing is just work we need to do to move on, and ..."

"Getting old is terminal!" a frantic voice interrupts me. "Before you know it, we'll go to sleep and never wake up this side of the fashion scene!"

"We'll never go to a shopping mall or dog park again!"

"Our houses will be covered with dust, and so will we!"

"My kids will rummage around in my file cabinets looking for money and jewelry and find my stash of pot."

"Don't worry, I'll head them off."

"Thanks."

More silence. Silence is golden only when you have children running around. At our ages, silence is a sign of pouting; self-pity; and perhaps the desire to go home and eat a package of cookies.

"Remember the angels, ladies," our angel advocate speaks up, just in time.

We respect the power of angels. We call on them for everything from forgiving ourselves for gossiping, to loosening a screw on a home project, to finding a lost sales slip. They are all around us, helping us through tax audits, colonoscopies, and remembering the name of someone we once considered our best friend.

"Okay, what are our angels trying to tell us right now?" the advocate asks with a voice used for children and wayward disciples.

"We're not dead yet?"

"Stop using a magnifying mirror?"

"Be grateful?"

Who Are We, Really?

It's not that we're ungrateful—goodness, no!

We are the generation of gratitude journals, gratitude lists, gratitude prayers, and gratitude therapy, followed by the many lectures we have given our grandchildren on the importance of gratitude.

Speaking of our grandchildren, aside from our gratitude lectures, we do impress them. My grandchildren, for example, listen with wonder when I talk about buying our first house for only sixteen thousand dollars. My impersonation of Little Richard blows their minds. Their mouths hang open when they watch me roller-skate down a sidewalk. Most of all, they are amazed that I made it through high school without texting.

They are also impressed by all the "collector items" they spot around my house. I have promised to will them several things they are sure will turn a pretty penny someday, including my pig collection, the piano music I've been learning to play since I was nine, my wind-up alarm clock, my transistor radio, a phone with a cord, my pager, and some actual stationery and stamps. Oh yes, they also covet a book of Green Stamps, which was a collector's item willed to me by my mother.

The trouble is, I sometimes I think *I* am becoming a collector's item myself, especially when I hum "Zippity doo dah," write a thank-you note in longhand, or wear pantyhose with sandals.

Encounter Group Methods

This brings me back to the encounter group at hand.

When our minds wander far away, as mine has just done, the girls like to do what our therapists called "experiential exercises."

We may take turns falling backwards into the group's arms; or we may take turns talking to an empty chair, imagining someone who hurt us when we were children is sitting there. Then we give that person a real piece of our minds.

Or, we may talk to *ourselves* in the empty chair. For example, we can tell our younger selves how getting old is a good thing because we no longer have cramps, homework, or eyelashes for mascara to clump on.

If all else fails to cheer us up, we may draw our "lifelines," documenting all the major events in our lives on long sheets of butcher paper: *long, long* sheets of butcher paper.

Group Hugs

After we have had one of our encounter groups, we feel much better about our aching backs, painful corns, tennis elbows, failing eyesight, and even the cost of our tooth implants. We stand in a circle, and everyone gets a group hug and some positive feedback.

"I know what," our leader says. "Before our group hug, let's give each other some positive feedback with the 'talk behind your back' game.'"

The "talk behind your back" game, for those who were not fortunate enough to be in group therapy during the seventies, is simply an exercise in which everyone writes one (anonymous) compliment for each group member on a small piece of paper and tapes the kind words to the backs of the intended recipients. Each person then reads the words of praise bestowed on her back, to sniffles all around.

Not only does this game reveal how much we are loved; it also verifies how intact our vocabularies still are: *gracious, creative, sweet, trustworthy, smart, well dressed, sincere, loving, curious*—suddenly a particular word hangs in the air like a whisker on your chin: *youthful.*

"We're supposed to be honest," the recipient complains.

"I looked it up the other day," is the smug retort. "The dictionary says *youthful* applies to one who is, or appears to be, in the period between childhood and maturity."

"Between childhood and maturity," the recipient muses. "I like that!"

Suddenly our angel advocate stands apart, and we know she will soon recite:

"This moment we step forward into our futures!" she says, with a flourish of her lovely hand. "Our futures hold mysteries and secrets of untold wonder. We are no longer bound by things of the past. Yea, our spirits soar above the gravity of simple youth. We are and forever will be *free!*"

"I'll vote for that!" a voice chimes in.

"All in favor," someone says.

"Aye!" is the unanimous decision—as we fall into the best group hug since shag haircuts and bell-bottom pants!

Suddenly our angel advocate stands apart,
and we know she will soon recite.

Conclusion

The next time we peer into our makeup mirrors and feel compelled to lift the sides of our faces back into ponytails with rubber bands, we must remember this book and laugh together at gravity.

When a young girl at a checkout stand stares at our driver's license picture and says, "Wow, you were young then!" we must smile gracefully while secretly laughing our heads off at how she'll eat those words someday.

When summer comes again and we check our legs in a pair of shorts to see what winter has wrought, we can laugh out loud at the new spider veins and fallen calves. Gravity can't touch the way we kick up our heels!

When we awaken in the middle of the night wondering whatever happened to a full night's sleep, we must quietly slip out of our beds and steal off to our special corners. Then we must switch on the little book lights we have hidden there, along with our copies of this book. In a spirit of togetherness, we must not wake people as we laugh and yawn at gravity.

When we feel hopelessly old-fashioned, gasping at the sight of kids attempting to walk with their pants around their knees, we must remember: kids have a right to laugh at gravity too.

When we wonder what we will leave behind besides the footbaths given to us for Christmas and, therefore, ethically ours till the end; the "permanent" lipsticks that turn our lips to sandpaper; and the collections of ugly purses that have filled the best parts of our closets since we can remember; let's get out our memoir books and write the stories of these things, so our families can join us in laughing at gravity long after we're gone.

Three, two, one; *we have liftoff*—laughing all the way!

Photo Op

An ex-chorus girl, this eighty-something diva
can only be called "delicious."

*One member of our troupe is a retired high-fashion model
who dramatically quotes lines from the theatre.*

Our beautiful German gourmet is a world traveler who introduces us to artisan bread with butter and pesto.

Only other women know how it feels. How what feels? Everything we need to talk about!

Shopping is the hunting and gathering of modern womanhood.

*The day we retire, we begin calling our women
friends "honey," "dear," and "sweetie."*

We must expand our outlets for lively conversation.

If we never trusted other women, now is the time to get over it.

Collections remind us of the children living secretly in our aging bodies.

*You may feel old in a class of nine-year-olds at a
recital, but just think—you are the only one who can
pop a tranquiller before it's your turn to play.*

I can't say I actually love my new car yet, but I know it will come in time.

Three, two, one; we have liftoff—laughing all the way!

About the Author

Sheila Lopez is a sixtyish, retired psychotherapist, who has discovered that aging is funny.

"My retired gal-pals and I disturb other diners with our giggling," she says. "It's really shameful!"

Sheila lives in a home with a license plate in Auburn, California.